GINGER SNAP'S COOKIE BOOK

A Sugar and Spice Adventure

by Alison Saeger Panik

Scholastic Inc.

New York Toronto London Auckland Sydney Mexico City New Delhi Hong Kong Buenos Aires

ISBN 0-439-70467-7

Designer: Emily Muschinske
Illustrations: Lisa and Terry Workman
Photographs: Alison Saeger Panik

12 11 10 9 8 7 6 5 4 3 2 1   4 5 6 7 8 9/0

Printed in the U.S.A.
First Scholastic printing, January 2005

TABLE OF CONTENTS

Get Ready for a COOKIES AND CRAFTS ADVENTURE!

Hi, it's me, Strawberry Shortcake, and my berry special friend, Ginger Snap.

Welcome to the village of Cookie Corners! I'm a cookie chef and an inventor. I'm always thinking of new ideas for the perfect cookie. Even my house and bakery are made out of cookies!

Let's have fun baking cookies and making cookie crafts together!

My cute pet, Chocolate Chipmunk, will join us, too. Are you ready? Grab your Cookie Craft Kit and let's get started!

Ginger Snap and Strawberry Shortcake's Tips for Getting Started

1. It's a berry good idea to gather everything you need before you begin a project or recipe.

2. Invite a friend or grown-up to join you. Everything is twice as much fun when it's shared!

3. Whenever you see this symbol throughout the book, it means that you can find what you need in your craft kit.

4. You can find many of the materials for the projects in the book around your house. Check a grocery or craft store for supplies that you don't have.

5. Some activities in the book have this symbol. It means you will need a grown-up's help for the project.

Getting Ready to Make Cookies

1. **Before you make a recipe, wash your hands with soap and warm water.**

2. **Wear an apron or a smock to keep your clothes clean and neat.**

3. **Before rolling out cookie dough or making cookie shapes, wipe the table or counter with a warm soapy cloth, then dry it with a clean towel.**

4. **Sprinkle a little flour on the counter before rolling or shaping cookie dough so it doesn't stick. You can also rub flour on cookie cutters and rolling pins, too.**

5. **Ask a grown-up to preheat the oven 10–15 minutes before you're ready to bake the cookies. Remember—ovens are for grown-ups only.**

The Berry Best Ingredients

- **Butter (or margarine) should be at room temperature, not cold. Set your butter out about 20–30 minutes before you start making your recipe.**

- **Large eggs make the best cookies.**

- **The cookies in this book use white, all-purpose flour.**

- **Sugar can be white, brown, or powdered. White sugar looks like salt. Brown sugar is moist and should be packed into a measuring cup by pressing down on top with a spoon. Powdered sugar is light and fluffy like powder.**

- **Vanilla extract is a flavoring made from vanilla beans. It makes a recipe taste good, but it doesn't taste good by itself.**

Turn the page to color pretty pictures with crayons and cookie cutters!

Colorful Cookie Cutter Crayon Designs

Ginger Snap and I use cookie cutters to draw these pretty pictures!

What You Need

- Construction paper (any color)
- Cookie cutter stencil
- Gingerbread man cookie cutter
- Crayons

1. Lay down a sheet of construction paper the tall way. Which shape would you like to draw? A gingerbread man? A star, flower, or heart? You decide!

2. Place your stencil (for the star, flower, or heart) or your cookie cutter (for the gingerbread man) on the center of your paper. Trace around the stencil or cookie cutter with a crayon. Lift it up to see your shape!

3. **Choose another crayon color, and trace around the crayon outline again. You will have two crayon outlines around your shape.**

4. **Keep tracing around the crayon outlines with different colors. Use as many colors as you like. Can you make six, seven, or eight outlines?**

5. **Now color the inside of the shape with crayons. Add designs, if you like.**

Here's More:

- Cut out the whole design and tape it onto a card or wrapped gift!
- Make lots of designs on one large piece of paper to create a colorful placemat.

Turn the page to bake some sunny cookie shapes!

What You Need

- Pencil
- Gingerbread man cookie cutter
- Cookie cutter stencil
- 1 sheet of dark blue, black, or purple construction paper
- Scissors
- 1 sheet of any color construction paper (not the fade-less kind)
- Tape
- Small rocks or paperweights

Sun-baked Cookie Shapes

You can make cookies—in a cookie picture—that are baked by the sun!

1. Use a pencil to trace around your gingerbread man cookie cutter and stencil shapes on the sheet of dark paper. Make lots of cookie shapes!

2. Cut out the cookie shapes with scissors.

3. **Arrange the cut-outs on the other sheet of colored paper, any way you like.**

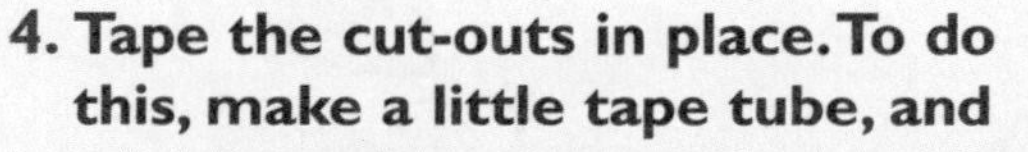

4. **Tape the cut-outs in place. To do this, make a little tape tube, and stick it under a cut-out. Then press the cut-out onto the paper.**

5. **Place the paper with the taped cut-outs on a sunny windowsill. Put a few small rocks or paperweights in the corners, so that the paper doesn't blow away.**

6. **"Bake" your cookies in the sun for two days. Carefully pull off the cut-outs. Can you see your cookie shapes on the paper?**

Here's More: You can "bake" your cut-outs longer if you like. Each extra day of baking in the sun will make the cookie shapes stand out more brightly!

Turn the page to make a berry special cookie chain!

Ginger Snap's Cute Cookie Chain

Ginger Snap makes these cookie chains to decorate a "cookie corner" in every room of her house!

What You Need

- 8 Colorful Cookie Cutter Crayon Designs (from pages 6–7)
- Scissors
- 4–5 feet of ribbon or string
- Tape

1. Cut around each Colorful Cookie Cutter Crayon Design with scissors.

2. Fold back the top of each shape about an inch from the edge. Snip two slits 1/2-inch apart into the fold. Each snip should be about 1/4-inch deep.

3. Take one shape and push the end of the ribbon or string through the back of one slit, so the ribbon comes out in the front.

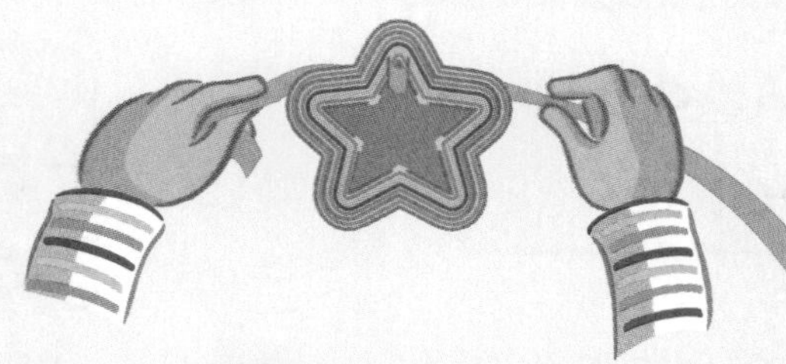

4. Push the ribbon or string end through the other slit, so that it comes out from the back of the shape. Slide the shape to the farthest end of the ribbon or string.

5. Repeat steps 3 and 4 to put the rest of your shapes on the ribbon or string. Space your shapes out evenly. Tape the shapes to the ribbon or string on the back, to keep them in place.

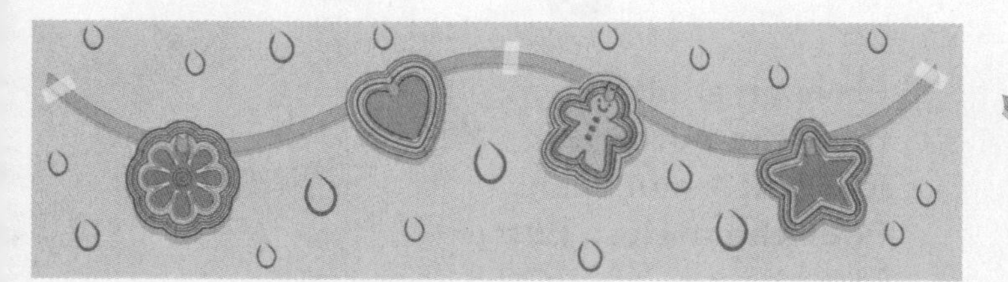

6. Hang your Cute Cookie Chain on the wall—in your bedroom, or in your play room.

Here's More:

- Make lots of cookie chains to decorate for a party!
- Design a cookie chain with the letters of your name written on the cookies. Hang your name chain on the door to your room!

Turn the page to make kisses and hugs taste yummy!

Kisses and Hugs Cookies

X is the symbol for a kiss.
O is the symbol for a hug!

What You Need

- Cooking spray
- 3 1/4 cup flour
- 3/4 cup sugar
- 3 teaspoons baking powder
- 1/2 cup butter or margarine
- 3 eggs
- 1/2 teaspoon vanilla
- Utensils: Large bowl, measuring cups and spoons, small saucepan, wooden spoons, cookie sheet

Makes: 3 dozen cookies

1. Spray a cookie sheet with cooking spray. Ask an adult to preheat the oven to 375°F.

2. Pour the flour, sugar, and baking powder into a large bowl.

3. Have an adult melt the butter in a small saucepan. Pour the melted butter into the large bowl that has the flour mixture. Add the eggs and the vanilla, and stir until you have formed dough.

4. Knead the dough with your hands in the bowl to form a ball.

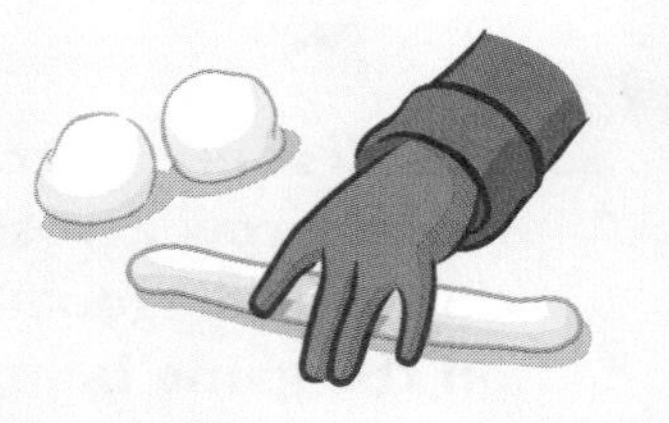

5. Pull off a piece of dough about the size of a strawberry. Roll the dough on the table with your hands to make a rope.

6. Cross two 3-inch pieces of rope to make an X. To make an O, shape a 5-inch piece of rope into a circle. Place the X's and O's on the greased cookie sheet. Keep making X's and O's until you run out of dough.

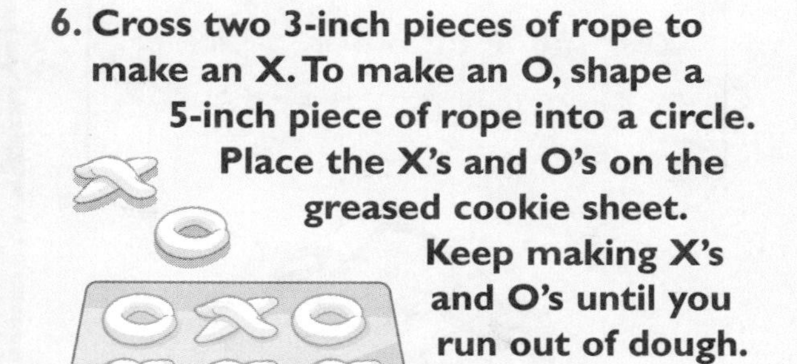

7. Ask an adult to bake your cookies in the oven for 5–7 minutes, or until they're golden around the edges. An adult should remove the cookie sheet from the oven. Let the cookies cool before playing with them (see page 14) or eating them.

Turn the page to play a game with your Kisses and Hugs Cookies!

Cookie Tic-Tac-Toe

Use your Kisses and Hugs Cookies to play this fun game with a friend!

What You Need

- Paper towels
- 4 pieces of licorice
- 5 X cookies (see page 12)
- 5 O cookies (see page 12)
- 2 Berry Sweet Players

1. Make a game board to play tic-tac-toe by laying four pieces of licorice on a paper towel, as shown.

2. Each player chooses X's or O's. Both players take turns putting one of their cookies in a space on the game board.

3. The first player to make a row across, down, or diagonally on the game board wins!

Here's More: Put the cookies, licorice, and a folded paper towel in a sealable bag, and you're set to go! Take your game along on a picnic, or on a visit to a friend's house.

Look at the next page to make one of Ginger Snap's favorite cookies!

Ginger Snap's Berry Best Ginger Cookies

You can make a yummylicious gingerbread man just like the one on Ginger Snap's hat!

What You Need

- 1 cup butter, softened
- 1 ½ cups sugar
- 2 tablespoons honey
- 1 egg
- 2 ½ cups flour
- 1 teaspoon baking soda
- 2 teaspoons ground cinnamon
- 2 teaspoons ground ginger
- Cooking spray
- Rolling pin
- Gingerbread man cookie cutter
- Utensils: 2 large bowls, wooden spoons, measuring cups and spoons, cookie sheets, plastic wrap, drinking glass, spatula, wire rack or paper towels

Makes: 2–3 dozen cookies

1. In a large bowl, combine the softened butter, sugar, and honey until they're smooth and creamy. Then add the egg and stir until everything is mixed.

2. In a second large bowl, combine the flour, baking soda, cinnamon, and ginger. Stir this mixture into the butter mixture in the first bowl, until you have dough.

(continues)

3. Press the dough in the bowl with your hands to form a big ball. Cover the bowl with plastic wrap and put it in the refrigerator for at least 30 minutes.

4. An adult should preheat the oven to 375°F. Spray the cookie sheets with cooking spray.

5. Sprinkle a little flour on a clean table and on the rolling pin. Put the dough on the floured table and flatten it with your hands. Use your rolling pin to roll the dough out about 1/4-inch thick.

6. To make gingerbread man cookies, place your gingerbread man cookie cutter on the dough and press down. Lift the cutter straight up to see your gingerbread man!

7. To make round cookies, place a drinking glass upside-down on the flattened dough. Press down on the bottom of the glass, and lift it straight up. Make as many shapes as you can fit on your dough.

8. Now carefully take away all the extra dough around the shapes. Use a spatula to place the cookie shapes $1\frac{1}{2}$-inches apart on the cookie sheets.

9. Press the leftover dough into a ball again. Repeat steps 5–9 until you've used up all your cookie dough.

Ginger Snap's Baking Tip:
Check your cookies after 5 or 6 minutes. If you like your cookies chewy, they can come out of the oven a little early. If you like crispy cookies, bake them a little longer.

10. Ask an adult to bake your cookies for 8 minutes in the preheated oven. After an adult takes the cookies out of the oven, allow them to cool for 5 minutes. Then have an adult help you move them to a wire rack or paper towel to cool completely.

Turn the page to paint your cookies with colorful frosting!

Fun Finger Paint Frosting

This colorful frosting makes Ginger Snap's cookies look berry pretty!

1. Measure the powdered sugar and milk into a bowl. Stir until the frosting is smooth (it should be a little thicker than school glue). If the frosting is runny, add a little more sugar and stir again.

What You Need

- 2 cups powdered sugar
- Ginger Cookies (see pages 15–17)
- 4 tablespoons milk
- Food coloring (optional)
- Utensils: Measuring cups and spoons, bowls, wooden spoon

Makes: 2 cups of frosting

2. To paint, dip your finger in the frosting and spread it over a cookie (like the Ginger Cookies you made on pages 15–17).

3. To make colored frosting, divide the white frosting into two bowls. Add food coloring, one drop at a time, to each bowl and stir. Keep adding food coloring until the frosting is the color you like.

4. To decorate your cookies, spread one frosting color on each cookie. Paint frosting designs—like dots, stripes, and swirls—with a different colored frosting. The frosting will dry in about 15 minutes.

Cookie Designs

To make a dot, dab your finger in frosting, place it on the cookie, and quickly lift your finger.

To make stripes, put frosting on your finger, and then drag it across the cookie to make a line.

To make a swirl, dab your finger on the cookie like you're making a dot, then move your finger around the dot in circles.

Turn the page for a fun cookie puzzle!

Cookie Collecting!

Do you love cookies as much as Ginger Snap does? Try this maze and see!

Follow the path of the maze from START to FINISH with your finger. **Count each cookie you pass along the way. Add up the cookies to see how many you've collected. Can you collect all the cookies without going over any part of the maze twice?**

Here's More: Try traveling different ways to collect different numbers of cookies!

- Can you go from START to FINISH and collect exactly 3 cookies?
- Can you go from START to FINISH and collect exactly 5 cookies?
- Can you go from START to FINISH and collect exactly 8 cookies?

Berry Funny

Q: Why don't eggs tell jokes?

A: They'd crack each other up!

Turn to page 38 for the answers.

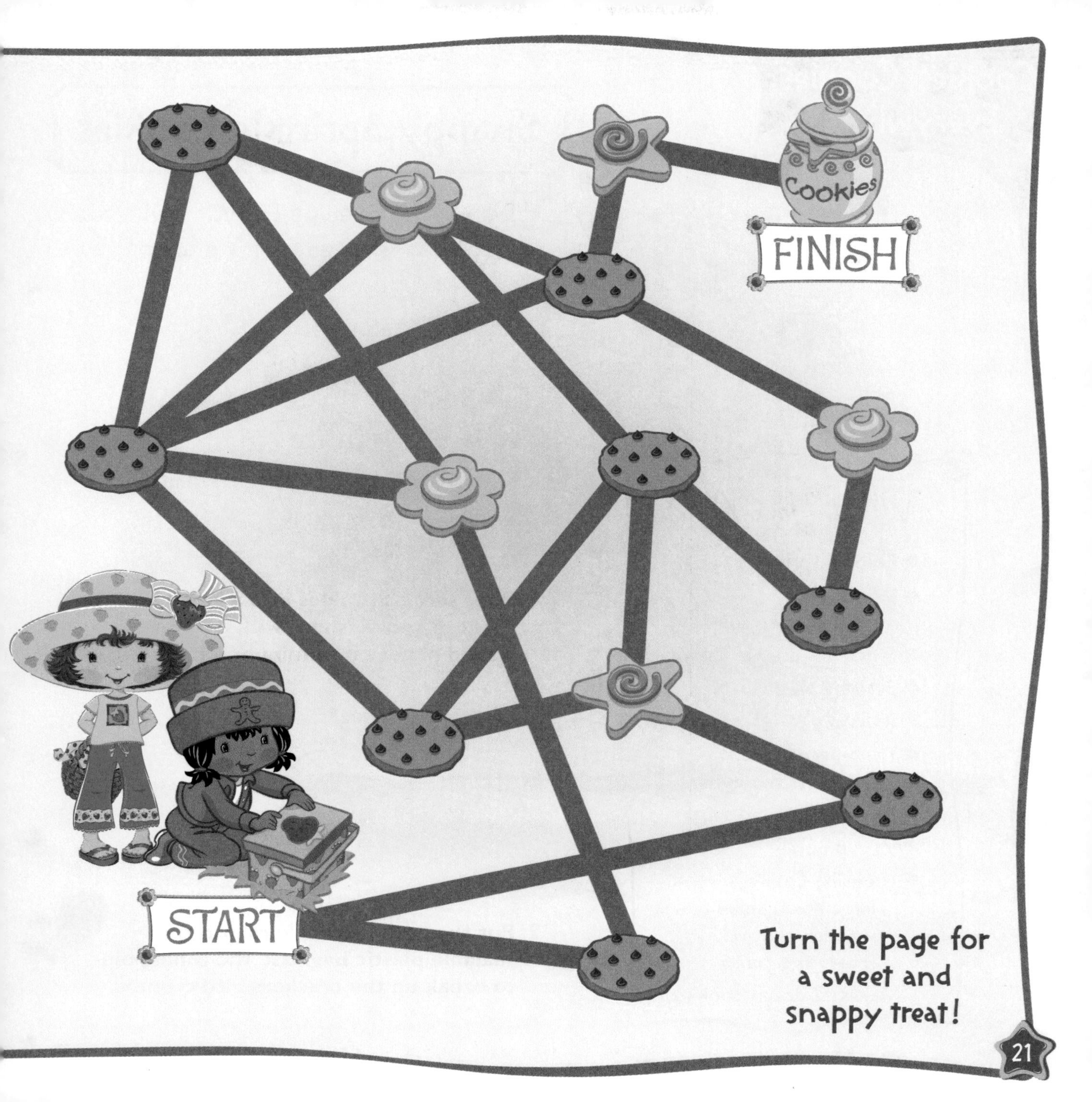

Turn the page for
a sweet and
snappy treat!

Snappy Sprinkle Cookies

This no-bake recipe for yummylicious cookies is so easy—it's a snap!

What You Need

- Colored sprinkles
- Waxed paper or aluminum foil
- 5 graham cracker sheets
- Sealable plastic bag
- Rolling pin
- 1 cup peanut butter (or other nut butter)
- 1/2 cup powdered sugar
- 1/4 cup honey
- Utensils: Cookie sheet, large bowl, small bowl, wooden spoon, measuring cups

Makes: 2 dozen cookies

1. Pour some sprinkles into a small bowl. Cover a cookie sheet with a piece of waxed paper or aluminum foil.

2. Put the graham crackers into the sealable plastic bag. Use the rolling pin to break up the crackers into crumbs.

3. Pour the graham cracker crumbs into a large bowl. Add the peanut butter, powdered sugar, and honey. Stir until all the ingredients are combined.

4. Spoon out a strawberry-sized mound of dough. Shape the dough into a ball by rolling the dough between your palms.

5. Roll the ball in the colored sprinkles. Place the ball on the cookie sheet. Repeat steps 4 and 5 until you run out of dough.

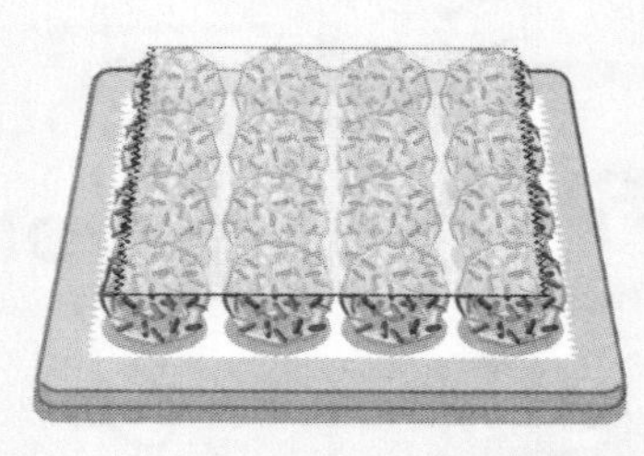

6. Place a piece of waxed paper or foil over the cookies and place them in the refrigerator for 15 minutes to chill. Take them out of the refrigerator and enjoy!

Here's More: If you don't have colored sprinkles, you can roll the cookies in mini-chocolate chips, granola, or coconut, or you can crush some of your favorite cereal for an extra snappy crunch!

Turn the page to bake more delicious cookies!

Chocolate Chipmunk's Favorite Oatmeal Cookies

Ginger Snap named these cookies after her favorite pet pal Chocolate Chipmunk!

What You Need

- 3 cups rolled oats
- 1 cup milk
- 2 cups flour
- 1 teaspoon baking soda
- 1 teaspoon salt
- 1 cup butter or margarine, softened
- 1 cup brown sugar
- ½ cup white sugar
- 2 eggs
- 1 teaspoon vanilla extract
- 1 cup semi-sweet chocolate chips
- Utensils: 3 bowls, wooden spoons, measuring cups and spoons, spoon, cookie sheet

Makes: 3 dozen cookies

1. Ask an adult to preheat the oven to 350°F. Pour the rolled oats into a bowl. Add the milk and stir. Let the oatmeal soak for 10 minutes.

2. Stir together the flour, baking soda, and salt in a second bowl.

3. In a third bowl, mix together the butter or margarine, brown sugar, and white sugar. Add the eggs and vanilla, and stir.

4. Add the flour mixture to the butter mixture. Stir in the oat mixture. Pour in the chocolate chips, and mix some more.

5. Scoop spoonfuls of dough onto a cookie sheet. Place the scoops of cookie dough 1–2 inches apart.

6. Ask an adult to bake the cookies for 12–15 minutes, or until the cookies are golden brown around the edges. Let cool on the cookie sheet before eating.

Turn the page to make a cookie-filled plate that you can give as a gift!

Ginger Snap's Berry Cute Cookie Plate

You can wrap up cookies to give to your friends and family, just like Ginger Snap does!

What You Need

- Cellophane sheets (pink, purple, and yellow)
- 9-inch disposable plate (use 3 paper plates stacked together to make a stronger plate)
- Cookies (home-made or from the store)
- Rubber band
- Scissors
- Pink ribbon
- Yellow rickrack

1. Lay out two sheets of cellophane in the shape of a big X. Lay the third sheet across the X so all the sheets look like a star, as shown.

2. Place the plate in the middle of the star. Arrange your cookies on the plate.

3. Pull up all of the ends of the cellophane and grip them in place.

4. Wrap a rubber band around the cellophane ends to hold them together.

5. Cut a piece of ribbon and a piece of rickrack (about 18 inches each). Tie the ribbon and rickrack around the rubber band on the cookie plate.

Turn the page for a jar of cookies just for you!

Ginger Snap's Cookie Jar

You can make a cookie container of your very own to keep all your favorite cookies—until you eat them, of course!

What You Need

- 1 empty container with a lid (like an oatmeal or drink mix container)
- Construction paper (blue and brown)
- Ruler
- Pencil
- Scissors
- Glue
- Tape
- Pink ribbon
- Yellow rickrack
- Gingerbread man cookie cutter
- Crayons

1. Lay your container down on top of a sheet of blue construction paper. Use a ruler and pencil to measure a strip of paper that's as long as the container. Cut it out. You might need to use two sheets of paper if you have a big container.

2. Glue the paper strip to the container. Use tape to hold the edges down, if you need to.

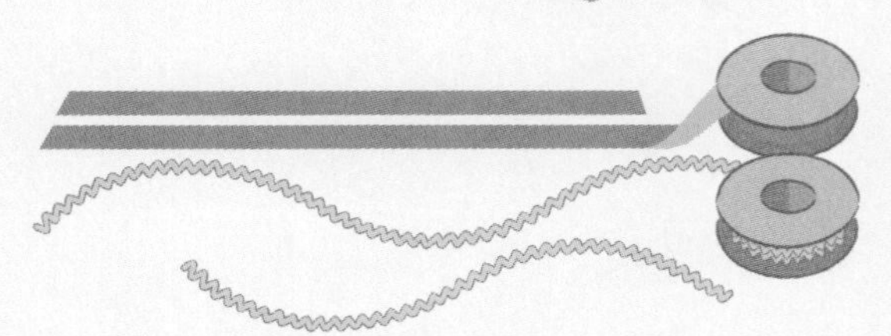

3. Wrap the pink ribbon around the top of the container so the ends overlap a little. Cut off any extra ribbon. Use this ribbon to measure and cut another piece of ribbon and two pieces of rickrack, all the same length.

4. Glue the two pieces of ribbon around the top and bottom of the container. Glue the rickrack over the ribbon.

5. Trace around the gingerbread man cookie cutter on a sheet of brown construction paper with a pencil. Use crayons to decorate the shape.

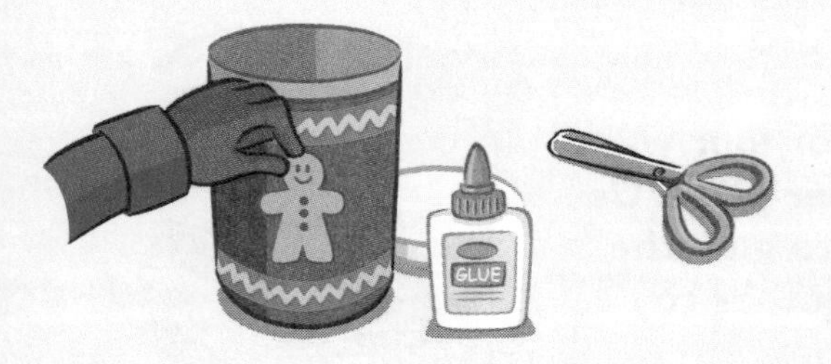

6. Cut out the shape and glue it to the front of your container.

Here's More: Seal the lid tightly on your cookie jar so the cookies stay fresh. If your lid doesn't fit tightly, put a piece of aluminum foil over the top of the container before putting on the lid.

Turn the page to build a cookie house just like Ginger Snap's!

Ginger Snap's Cookie Cottage

Where does everyone live in Ginger Snap's tiny village of Cookie Corners? In cute cookie cottages, of course!

What You Need

- Toothpick
- 1 cup Fun Finger Paint Frosting (see pages 18–19)
- 1 package of sugar wafer cookies
- Paper plate
- Optional: Candy, chocolate chip cookies (to decorate your cottage)

1. To make the walls of your cookie cottage, use a toothpick to put frosting on one side of a sugar wafer. Press another wafer into the frosting, so the two wafers stick together.

2. "Glue" another wafer on to your wall with frosting so it's three wafers wide. Repeat steps 1 and 2 three more times to make three more walls.

3. Place your four walls on a paper plate. Use frosting to glue the walls together to make a box.

4. To make your cottage's roof, glue two wafers to make an upside-down V on top of the box. Keep gluing on wafers until the walls are totally covered with a roof.

5. Break two sugar wafers into three pieces each. Glue the pieces on the sides of the roof to cover the gaps.

6. Use candies and other cookies to add doors and windows. Use frosting to glue the candy or cookies into place. Decorate your cottage with more candy, if you like.

Here's More: You can make a cookie tree for your cookie cottage! Break a sugar wafer in half, and glue a chocolate chip cookie to one end. Glue the tree to the bottom of the paper plate next to your house.

Turn the page to create a cookie craft you can both wear and eat!

Ginger Snap's Sweet Cookie Necklace

This cookie necklace is as sweet to wear as it is to eat!

What You Need

- 6 licorice strings
- 3 round, store-bought cookies with holes in the center

1. Tie three licorice strings together to make one long string with two knots in it.

2. Put one licorice string through the hole in each of the three cookies. Tie one cookie in the middle of the long string.

3. Tie the other two cookies beside each knot. Now your cookie necklace is ready to wear!

Here's More: Carefully tie the ends of the necklace around your neck. Once you're finished wearing your necklace, you can eat the cookies and licorice as a snack!

Look at the next page to create a fun cookie dunking game!

Ginger Snap's Cookie Caps

Make these Cookie Caps to play the Cookies and Milk Dunking Game!

What You Need

- Small plastic lids or caps from milk or orange juice containers
- Paper
- Colored pencils
- Scissors
- School glue

1. Trace around each cap on a piece of paper with a colored pencil to make a circle.

2. Color each paper circle to look like a cookie. What kind of cookies will you draw? It's up to you!

3. Cut out each cookie circle with scissors and glue each one onto a cap.

Here's More: Make two sets of matching cookie caps to play cookie checkers on a checkers game board.

Turn the page to play the Cookies and Milk Dunking Game!

Ginger Snap's Cookies and Milk Dunking Game

Milk loves freshly baked cookies! Use the Cookie Caps you made on page 33 to play this yummy tossing game!

What You Need

- 10 Cookie Caps (see page 33)
- An adult to help you count your points
- 2 Berry Sweet Players

1. Lay your book on the floor with these two pages open. Both players should stand one big step away from the book and sit down.
2. Decide who goes first. Player 1 tosses five Cookie Caps (one at a time) onto the playing board, trying to land her caps on the glasses of milk.
3. Once Player 1 runs out of caps, she counts up the points she's earned (on the milk glasses), and then takes her caps off the board. Then it's Player 2's turn.
4. Once both players have taken a turn, whoever has the most points wins!

Here's More: See whether you can toss your Cookie Caps just right so you get the same number of points as your friend!

Turn the page to see where Ginger Snap keeps the tools for her amazing cookie-making machine!

Ginger Snap's Toolbox

Ginger Snap carries her inventing tools in a special toolbox just like this one.

What You Need

- Aluminum foil
- 1 empty tissue box (the kind with an opening on the top)
- Tape
- Cookie cutter stencil
- Construction paper
- Crayons
- Scissors
- Pink ribbon

1. Tear off a large sheet of aluminum foil and wrap it around the tissue box. Press the foil around the edges of the top opening, and use tape to attach the ends of the foil to the box.

2. Trace the cookie cutter stencil on the sheet of construction paper with a crayon. Trace as many shapes as you like. Color the shapes, then cut them out.

3. **Roll a piece of tape so the sticky side faces out. Press the tape roll on the back of a shape and stick the shape onto the box.**

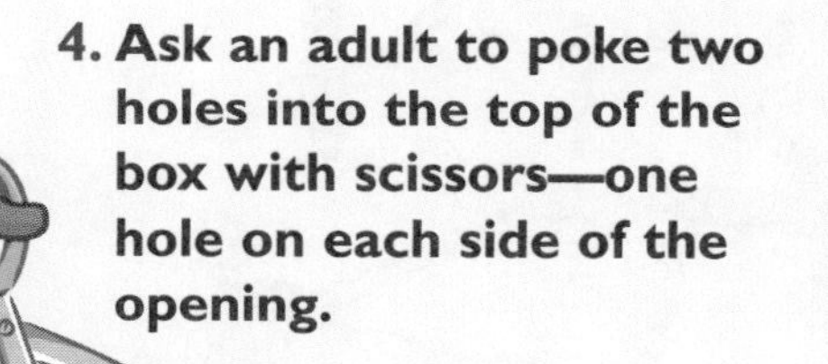

4. **Ask an adult to poke two holes into the top of the box with scissors—one hole on each side of the opening.**

5. **Cut a piece of ribbon (about 15 inches) to make a handle that reaches from one hole to the other. Push the ends of the ribbon through the holes and tape them inside the opening.**

6. **Fill your toolbox with your favorite art tools like crayons, scissors, and paintbrushes!**

Here's More: Create the letters of your name on a sheet of construction paper. Cut out each letter and tape it to your box to spell your name!

Ginger Snap's Answer Page

Cookie Collecting!
(pages 20 and 21)

Here's how to collect all the cookies:

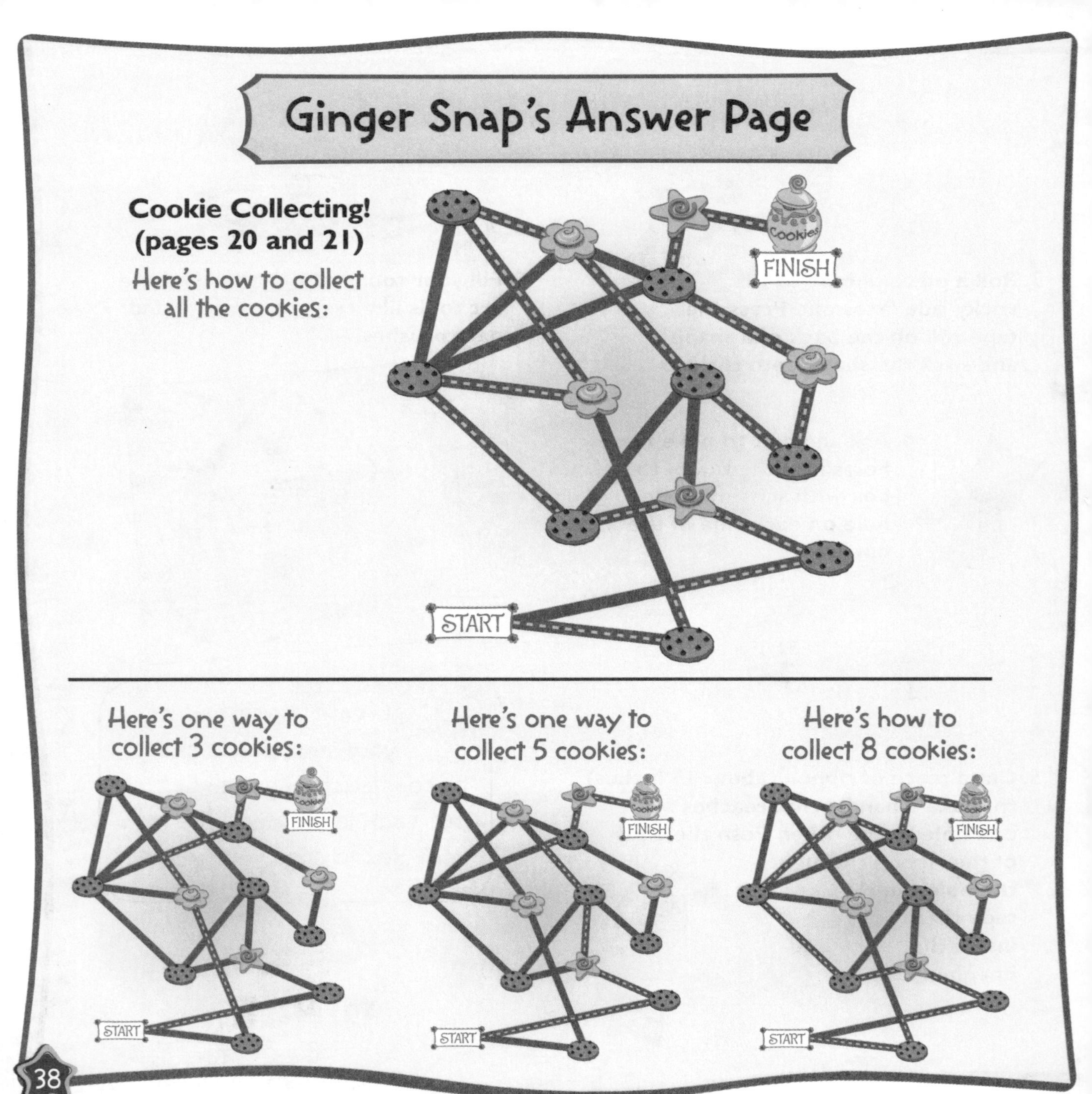

Here's one way to collect 3 cookies:

Here's one way to collect 5 cookies:

Here's how to collect 8 cookies:

More Sweet Strawberryland Adventures COMING SOON!

To Our Berry Special Friend,

Thank you for coming with us on our all-cookie adventure! We hope you had a good time in Cookie Corners baking cookies, tracing cookie pictures, and playing cookie games. It's always fun to get creative with you. Come back for more sweet treats and activities soon!

Your berry special friends,
Strawberry Shortcake,
GINGER SNAP, and
Chocolate Chipmunk